my itty-bitty bio

Alfred Nobel

Published in the United States of America by Cherry Lake Publishing
Ann Arbor, Michigan
www.cherrylakepublishing.com

Content Adviser: Ryan Emery Hughes, Doctoral Student, School of Education, University of Michigan
Reading Adviser: Marla Conn MS, Ed., Literacy specialist, Read-Ability, Inc.
Book Design: Jennifer Wahi
Illustrator: Jeff Bane

Photo Credits: ©Scanrail1/Shutterstock, 5; ©Pemaphoto/Shutterstock, 7; ©stevemart/Shutterstock, 9; ©Kristina Yu/Shutterstock, 11, 22; ©Georgios Kollidas/Dreamstime, 13; Fer Gregory/Shutterstock, 15, 23; ©Mark Agnor/Shutterstock, 17; ©Vladislav Gajic/Shutterstock, 19, ©Photos.com/Thinkstock, 21; Cover, 8, 14, 16, Jeff Bane; Various frames throughout, ©Shutterstock Images

Library of Congress Cataloging-in-Publication Data

Names: Devera, Czeena, author.
Title: Alfred Nobel / by Czeena Devera.
Other titles: My itty-bitty bio.
Description: Ann Arbor, MI : Cherry Lake Publishing, [2018] | Series: My itty-bitty bio | Audience: K to grade 3.
Identifiers: LCCN 2018003112| ISBN 9781534128859 (hardcover) | ISBN 9781534132054 (pbk.) | ISBN 9781534130555 (pdf) | ISBN 9781534133754 (hosted ebook)
Subjects: LCSH: Nobel, Alfred Bernhard, 1833-1896--Juvenile literature. | Chemical engineers--Sweden--Biography--Juvenile literature. | Dynamite--Juvenile literature. | Nobel Prizes--Juvenile literature.
Classification: LCC TP268.5.N7 D48 2018 | DDC 660.092 [B] --dc23
LC record available at https://lccn.loc.gov/2018003112

Printed in the United States of America
Corporate Graphics

table of contents

About the author: Czeena Devera grew up in the red-hot heat of Arizona surrounded by books. Her childhood bedroom had built-in bookshelves that were always too full. She now lives in Michigan with an even bigger library of books.

About the illustrator: Jeff Bane and his two business partners own a studio along the American River in Folsom, California, home of the 1849 Gold Rush. When Jeff's not sketching or illustrating for clients, he's either swimming or kayaking in the river to relax.

I was born in 1833 in Sweden.
I had three brothers.

My father was an **inventor** and builder. I also liked to invent and build things.

I liked learning.
I knew five languages.
I read **poetry**. I read books on **science**.

What languages would you like to learn?

I went to college in Paris. I met Ascanio Sobrero. He invented an **explosive**.

What would you like to invent?

I returned to Sweden. I studied the explosive. But it was not safe. The explosive hurt my younger brother.

I worked harder.
I made it safe.
I named it **dynamite**.

It helped speed up building. It helped save money.

I came up with an important **award**. I called it the Nobel Prize. I wanted people to work hard in science and art. A group was started to give out these awards.

What kind of group
would you start?

I died in 1896. I made more than 350 inventions. The first Nobel Prizes were awarded in 1901.

What would you like to ask me?

timeline

1850

1830

Born
1833

1866

1930

Died
1896

glossary

award (uh-WORD) something valuable given as a reward or honor

dynamite (DYE-nuh-mite) a very powerful explosive

explosive (ik-SPLOH-siv) something that can blow up

inventor (in-VENT-or) a person who thinks up or makes something new

poetry (POH-ih-tree) a collection of poems or writings that are organized in lines and often use words that have special sounds or meanings

science (SYE-uhns) the study of nature and the world we live in; a person who studies science is a scientist

index